THE GIFT

A Play in One Act

by

KENDALL MARLOWE

Dramatic Publishing
Woodstock, Illinois • England • Australia • New Zealand

*** NOTICE ***

IMPORTANT BILLING AND CREDIT REQUIREMENTS

All producers of the play *must* give credit to the author(s) of the play in all programs distributed in connection with performances of the play and in all instances in which the title of the play appears for purposes of advertising, publicizing or otherwise exploiting the play and/or a production. The name of the author(s) *must* also appear on a separate line, on which no other name appears, immediately following the title, and *must* appear in size of type not less than fifty percent the size of the title type. Biographical information on the author(s), if included in this book, may be used on all programs. *On all programs this notice must appear:*

THE GIFT was originally produced by Organic Theater Company, Chicago, on May 15, 1998, directed by Anna D. Shapiro, set and lighting design by Kevin Snow, costume design by Nancy Brundage, sound design by Joe Huppert, stage manager Leslie Kniskern, with the following cast:

Stephanie............................ KATIE CASSIS
Nick............................. CHRISTOPHER GROBE
Linda.............................. CYNTHIA JUDGE
Joseph .... ALAN WESTBROOK
Grandma .... LUCINA PAQUET

The play was commissioned by
Hope Cancer Care Network.

THE GIFT

A Play in One Act
For 7 Men and 6 Women (with doubling: 2m, 3w)

CHARACTERS

STEPHANIE................... the daughter, age 16

NICK............................. the son, age 14

LINDA .... the mother, age 40

JOSEPH......................... the father, age 42

GRANDMA .... Linda's mother, age 72

LIBRARIAN, NURSE, NURSE'S AIDE, ORDERLY,
DOCTOR, ADMINISTRATOR, CHAPLAIN,
MR. JOHNSON

NOTE ON DOUBLING

The play can be produced (and was originally produced) with just five actors. NICK plays the Nurse's Aide and the Doctor, JOSEPH plays the Orderly and the Chaplain, GRANDMA plays the Nurse and the Administrator. Mr. Johnson is referred to but not seen, and the Librarian's voice is recorded. In this interpretation of Stephanie's dreams, the characters assume other roles but do not lose their identity, just as, in a dream, your neighbor may seem to be your boss, but never stops being your neighbor.

SETTING

The action of the play should flow quickly from scene to scene—locations can be suggested by small pieces which may easily be moved or adjusted by the actors. The look is spare and selective, as in a dream. The family's minivan, for instance, may be five, tall wooden stools. The library may be a single bookcase. Dishes, clothing and personal items may be real, but perhaps food and drink are not. Movement of characters may be enough to suggest hallways, stairs and doors. Lighting to suggest setting, time, and mood.

THE GIFT

SCENE 1

(The parents' upstairs bedroom. Morning. A cluttered dressing table, facing upstage, with the suggestion of a large mirror. A bed nearby. Clothes, and shoes. As lights come up, we see STEPHANIE's face peer into the empty room, carefully.)

LINDA *(off)*. Stephanie!

(STEPHANIE sneaks into the room, her backpack in hand, straight toward her mother's dressing table. She is pretty in a sassy way—her clothes seem thrown on, her hair askew, but she carries an effortless chic that's the result of much effort and many adolescent hours in front of her mirror. Perhaps a designer T-shirt and tight black jeans. She moves to the dressing table, in front of the mirror, reaches for earrings, and begins to put them on.)

LINDA *(off)*. Stephanie, now! Let's move it!

(STEPHANIE looks back to check that no one's coming, then reaches for a necklace.)

STEPHANIE. Can I borrow your earrings, just once?
LINDA *(off)*. We talked about this, and what did I tell you?

(She has put on the necklace.)

STEPHANIE. I don't have anything to wear!

LINDA *(off)*. You're making the rest of the family late!

JOSEPH *(off)*. Stephanie, please!

(She reaches for a pair of shoes, throws them on, and strikes a pose in the mirror to test the shoes. Throws them off, tries another pair with higher heels, and another pose. Perfect. Rummages through her bag, mistakenly pulls out a pack of cigarettes, looks to the door to see she hasn't been discovered, and quickly sets the cigarettes down. Searches again, finds lipstick, begins to put it on— wrong color. She quickly rubs it off with the back of her hand. Rummages through things on the table, grabs another color, tests it, then carefully outlines her lips. Her lips strike a pose.)

JOSEPH *(off)*. Stephanie, let's go!

NICK *(off)*. If you make me late, Steph, I'm gonna kill you!

(She notices and picks up a framed picture. She studies it, then hurriedly reaches for three fitted jackets. Bright and sexy, they're in green, red and gold.)

STEPHANIE. Mom, can I borrow one of your jackets, just once?

LINDA *(off)*. No, Stephanie. Please, just not the gold one ...

(She drops the other two on the floor and jumps into the gold one. Hands on hips, she gives the mirror a look, to test her powers. Perfect.)

JOSEPH *(off)*. Stephanie, this minute, we're going—let's go!

STEPHANIE *(running out, leaving the cigarettes on the dressing table)*. All right, what's your problem?!

(She rushes down the stairs. Movement and noise as the family piles out of the house toward the minivan. LINDA is attractive, but is harried and on edge. She tries hard to appear independent and worldly, but the burden of motherhood and career show through— she looks fractured, pulled-apart on this particular morning. JOSEPH has the kind and comfortable look of a happily married man, with an air of the well-earned fatigue that comes with parenthood. NICK wears his clothes as though they had been taped on— nothing quite fits, as each of his body parts has been growing, independently, at its own rate. Including his voice.)

NICK *(as they head toward the van)*. You've got to drop me at Dave's house.

LINDA *(to STEPHANIE)*. How did that happen? Look at your hair!

NICK. To finish our lab project.

JOSEPH. I've got to get to work, Linda, I can't be late.

LINDA. I know. Dave's house. To work. *(To STEPH-ANIE.)* I only hope, someday, that you'll use your head—you've got one—and even though you don't *care* about anyone else, you'll think—"there are other people in this family, they have lives, too—I should think of them, too."

STEPHANIE. I'm not talking about any of this. I'm not a kid.

(As they get in the minivan.)

NICK. It's due fourth period. Our lab project. We mix the stuff up in Dave's basement, then put it in the oven.

JOSEPH. Linda, you might have to drop me first. *(To NICK.)* What stuff?

NICK. Chemistry, Dad. Experiments, reactions. Duh!

LINDA. Seat belts!

(They all pile in—LINDA driving, STEPHANIE beating NICK to the front seat. NICK and JOSEPH in the back.)

STEPHANIE. Whatever with your reactions. Mom, you have to drop me first at school. It's important.

LINDA. Stephanie—

NICK. No way!

STEPHANIE. Shut up, freshman.

LINDA. Please—just today—let's be a family. First, we get your grandmother.

STEPHANIE. No!

LINDA. We get her, we drop your father. Drop her, then to Dave's house, drop Nick.

STEPHANIE. I go first! Me!

LINDA. Drop Nick at Dave's house. Nicky, can you and Dave walk to the high school from there?

NICK. Sure.

JOSEPH. He's walking somewhere? Walking?

STEPHANIE. Never.

NICK. No. Dave has a car. He's a senior.

JOSEPH. You're taking senior chemistry?

NICK. It's easy, Dad. Whatever...

STEPHANIE. I can't believe I'll be late for all this. And what's with old Grandma, anyway?

LINDA. Stephanie.

NICK. What's your big hurry, Steph?

STEPHANIE. Shut up.

NICK. Wait a minute. *(Pause.)* I know.

STEPHANIE. Shut up.

NICK. Nice earrings, Steph. Lipstick, too.

STEPHANIE. Die.

LINDA *(looking)*. Stephanie, for God's sake, I told you about the jacket...

NICK. I know the hurry. Josh Martin might ask her to Homecoming. She sees him first period. He's about her last chance. Nice necklace.

STEPHANIE. As if that had anything to do with it!

JOSEPH. Steffi, why do you have to get dolled up like that? You'll go to the dance. Someone will— Why do you do that to your hair? Look at your mother—she doesn't have to do that—her hair is long and beautiful just like the day I met her. And I'll take her to any dance. *(The van slows, stops. JOSEPH leans forward to give LINDA a kiss.)*

LINDA. Joe, not here... *(He kisses her, then she begins to turn away.)* Oh, what the heck. *(She kisses him back, holding his head tightly.)* I love you.

STEPHANIE. God, you're embarrassing. I'm leaving this family.

(GRANDMA gets in the back, with help from NICK. She is stout and round and wears a nice old lady dress with matching purse. She is lively, and speaks with an Eastern European accent she has worked hard to overcome.)

GRANDMA. Who's kissing? Can I kiss, too? Ah, my little monkey! *(She kisses NICK's head. The van pulls forward.)*

NICK. Hi, Grandma.

GRANDMA. My princess! *(She reaches forward to rub STEPHANIE's head.)*

STEPHANIE. Grandma.

GRANDMA *(pulling back her hand)*. What did you do to your hair?

JOSEPH. She's looking for a boy. For Homecoming Dance.

STEPHANIE. Please!

JOSEPH. Which reminds me... *(Pulling a piece of paper from his briefcase.)* Any boy who wants to ask you to the dance... *(Showing STEPHANIE the paper.)* Any boy must first fill out this brief application.

GRANDMA. Now, Joseph...

STEPHANIE. God!

NICK. Ha-HA! *(He and JOSEPH laugh.)*

GRANDMA. When Joseph here asked your grandpa for Linda's hand, we didn't need any application. Your grandpa, God rest his soul, he asked Joseph some questions, and Joseph here was very nice. He was always nice to Grandpa.

JOSEPH. I was twenty-two. His wrists were bigger than my thighs. I wanted to stay alive. *(The van slows.)*

LINDA. Here we are, Joe. Love you.

GRANDMA. Goodbye, Joseph. (*She gives him a peck on the cheek.*)

NICK. Bye, Dad.

JOSEPH. Which reminds me, Stephanie—no football players.

STEPHANIE. Dad.

LINDA (*stopping him*). Honey—I love you.

JOSEPH. Bye, sweetheart. (*Kisses her.*) You all right?

LINDA. Sure. Fine.

JOSEPH. Say hi to your kids for me.

LINDA. No, actually ... not today. It's one of those ... teachers' in-service days. Meetings, I think. No blackboard, no second-grade kids, just ... meetings. You know.

JOSEPH. Then see you at home.

STEPHANIE. Come on!

JOSEPH (*stops, looking at STEPHANIE, chuckling*). Hey, you know—you know who she looks like—even with the clothes, the hair. It's just the look on her face ...

LINDA. No ...

JOSEPH. Yes. That October we met. Dead ringer.

STEPHANIE. As *if*!

JOSEPH. It's a compliment, Steffi—she swept me off my feet.

LINDA. Oh, please ...

STEPHANIE. As *if*! We are so *different*!

JOSEPH. Goodbye. (*He goes off. The van pulls away.*)

NICK. Hey, you should teach Mom's class someday, Steph.

GRANDMA. He's such a nice man.

STEPHANIE. Enough.

NICK. Second grade—just your speed. You might pick up some guys.

LINDA. Nicholas, stop it with your sister. She has a hard
day ahead.

GRANDMA *(to LINDA)*. Joseph. A nice man. He was always nice to your father. When your father asked me,
what do you think, I said— What do I know? I'm just
saying—he's a nice man. *(The van slows.)*

LINDA. Here we are, Mom. Take care. And give my best
to Berta.

GRANDMA. Oh, I will. *(Getting out.)* Goodbye, my little
monkey. Princess!

LINDA. Mother... You know I love you.

GRANDMA. Of course you do—don't be silly! Goodbye,
now. *(Waving.)* Bingo! Bingo! *(The van pulls away.)*

NICK. Mom.

LINDA. Yes, Nicholas, what. What now?

NICK. Mom, where's Grandma going?

LINDA. Where do you think? You know perfectly well
where she's going.

STEPHANIE. I'm going to be late. Faster!

NICK. Mom, where do they have bingo at seven-thirty on a
Monday morning?

LINDA. They don't.

STEPHANIE. I can't believe this. I'm running away from
home.

LINDA. Grandma meets her friend Berta at that diner for
coffee and a sweet roll. Then they go to the beauty
shop—not to get their hair done, just to talk. Bingo starts
at nine.

NICK. Too weird, Mom. *(The van slows.)*

LINDA. Here you go. *(NICK gets out. She stops him.)*
Sweetheart, Nicky. You know don't you, if anything
ever happened... I love you.

NICK (*backing away*). Sure, Mom, whatever. You OK? (*He steps away, as LINDA reaches out toward him. As he walks away:*) Hey, Steph, if nobody wants you, there's always the convent! They get free clothes! (*The van pulls away.*)

STEPHANIE. Why is everyone so mean to me? Always to *me*.

LINDA. Stephanie, please ...

STEPHANIE. Quick, Mom, faster. Let's go.

(*They drive for a moment, then LINDA takes a deep breath, pulling herself up. She looks behind, then slows the van and steers it to the side, stopping. Pause.*)

STEPHANIE. What are you doing?

LINDA (*beat*). Stephanie, you have your license with you, don't you?

STEPHANIE. Sure I do. Always.

LINDA. Good, I thought you would. Drive for me.

STEPHANIE. Awesome!

(*STEPHANIE bounds out of the van, and skips around the front to the driver's side, as LINDA slides slowly over to the passenger seat. STEPHANIE jumps in. As STEPHANIE reaches to put the van in gear, LINDA extends her arm first, blocking STEPHANIE. STEPHANIE looks at LINDA.*)

LINDA. Please understand, Stephanie. I've been so awful this morning— I didn't mean to be— I wanted to be so good, and now this. I'm so sorry.

STEPHANIE. Mom, what's the—

LINDA. You can't go to school today, Stephanie. I'm so sorry. I want more than anything for the nicest boy in the world to ask you to that dance today. Some boy that will make your daddy so proud.

STEPHANIE. Mom, I have to—

LINDA. But you can't. You can't go. Please...forgive me. I called the school and excused the absence. They won't expect you.

STEPHANIE. Mother, what do you think you're doing? I have to go!

LINDA. And whatever you do, don't tell your father. Please don't. I couldn't tell him— I couldn't do that to him. It will be nothing, and he won't have to know.

STEPHANIE. Mother...

LINDA. Remember when I went to the doctor last week? My regular visit, once a year.

STEPHANIE. Yeah, so—what does that have to do with anything?

LINDA. A week after you went, right?

STEPHANIE. I suppose. Now—

LINDA. Only I'm forty now. They gave me a mammogram. My first.

STEPHANIE (beat). Mother, what are you telling me—

LINDA. So today I'm going back. To a different doctor. By the hospital. (Beat.) And you're taking me. (Pause.) Please.

(Pause. STEPHANIE puts the van into gear, and it pulls away.)

Take a left at the light.

(She does. Pause. Turning to STEPHANIE.)

I'm so sorry. *(Lights fade.)*

SCENE 2

(The school library. Late afternoon. As lights come up, STEPHANIE is alone by a bookcase, surrounded by books—they're spread around her on the floor, and in her arms. She looks scattered and dazed. She's frantically searching.)

NOTE: The librarian's announcements on the loudspeaker may be read live, or may be recorded.

LIBRARIAN'S VOICE ON LOUDSPEAKER This library will close in five minutes. We will reopen tomorrow, first period. Please return all books to the circulation desk at this time. Please note that boys basketball tryouts scheduled for tonight have been moved from the field house to the main gym. Basketball tryouts at six o'clock in the main gym for all boys. This library is about to close.

(As STEPHANIE faces away, NICK enters, backing in, waving to someone. STEPHANIE's face is in the book.)

NICK. Yo, Dave—tomorrow! *(He collides with STEPH-ANIE, who is startled and drops her book.)*
STEPHANIE. Oh—
NICK. Yo, Sister. What are you doing here?

STEPHANIE. Nothing, I—

NICK. They said that you were sick, that you weren't in class.

STEPHANIE. Yeah, that's right. Sick. I was—

NICK. What happened? You're a mess.

STEPHANIE. What's a biopsy?

NICK. What?

STEPHANIE. A ... biopsy. People, like, get one. What does it do?

NICK. I don't know. What are you doing? *(He sees books.)*

STEPHANIE. Research, I'm ... writing a paper. It's over-due.

NICK. What about? *(He moves toward books, as she tries to hide them.)* Whoa. Disease central. Terminal. What are you doing—trying to find a cure for your personal-ity?

STEPHANIE *(grabbing him by the collar)*. Listen. You know about this stuff.

NICK. I took bio. I don't know— I aced it. Whatever.

STEPHANIE *(still holding him by the collar)*. Then tell me. Biopsy.

NICK. It's like ... a test. They take it out, they look at it, see what you've got. You sick or something?

STEPHANIE. People ... when they get that ... do they live? Is there any chance? Why would they do that if there wasn't any chance?

NICK. I don't know. *(Backing away.)* Hey, if you want me to write your paper, I'll do it. Twenty dollars a page.

STEPHANIE. No. Do they live?

NICK. I should get Dave to help you. He's a senior, gonna be pre-med. But he thinks you're cute, so he can't be that smart.

STEPHANIE. Can't you help me? What's malignant mean— I need to know. What's carcinoma.

NICK (*moving toward her, looking at her*). Hey what happened to you? You weren't sick, were you. Your face is a mess. Where were you—off with some guy or something?

(*STEPHANIE slaps him very hard across the face, knocking him back into the books. He reaches for his mouth, and staggers to his feet. He pulls his hand from his mouth, and sees blood.*)

Hey, what's the matter with you? You cut my lip—are you crazy? (*He starts to walk away.*) Wait till Dad hears about this ... (*He turns to go. She lunges toward him, and pulls him back.*)

STEPHANIE. No. Please. I beg you. You can't tell Dad. Anything. Nick. (*She dives into his arms, clutching him, in tears.*) I'm your sister. Please don't tell. He can't know anything. I beg you.

NICK (*pulling away, more gently*). OK, OK. (*Beat.*) I won't tell. I don't know what's the matter with you Steph, but ... take a pill. (*Beat.*) It's OK. I won't tell. (*He backs away.*)

LIBRARIAN'S VOICE ON LOUDSPEAKER. This library is now closed. Please return all books and exit through the main door. This library is now closed.

(*NICK leaves, as STEPHANIE, on her knees, is alone. Lights fade.*)

SCENE 3

(The parents' bedroom. JOSEPH stands with his back to the closed door, trying to contain LINDA, who is upset and waving around a stack of papers.)

LINDA. I didn't want to have to tell you, even about the appointment. I felt like such a criminal. I won't have to tell him, it's nothing. It's nothing, so he won't need to know. He has his job, the family, he has all he can do, don't give him this and frighten him, too. It would be nothing. And now this. *(She indicates the papers.)*

JOSEPH. I understand. You tried to protect me.

LINDA. What have I done to myself? What have I done to you—to the kids!

JOSEPH. Nothing at all. You're not to blame—

LINDA. That's what he said. The doctor.

JOSEPH. Of course.

LINDA. We talked about risk. About behavior, eating habits, family history...

STEPHANIE *(off)*. Mom? Dad!

LINDA. Why, you don't *have* any of the classical risk factors, he said, like he was almost a little disappointed. Well, I worry a little, I said—you know how life is— maybe I drink a little too much wine, maybe my diet... But Linda, he said, I've known you what—ten years? You've been the picture of health—and you're manic about nutrition—the way you feed your family...

STEPHANIE *(off)*. Mom, are you up there?

LINDA. So don't kick yourself about a glass of wine at age forty. What happened, happened—it doesn't mean you're to blame.

JOSEPH. Just like I said!

LINDA. Besides, he said, those carcinogens—that kind of exposure—excessive drinking, smoking, the high-fat diet —those kind of things matter most to *young* women— the beginning of adolescence to first pregnancy—that's the real danger period, or so the studies say. The body's so sensitive then, or so it seems. Oh, I said. Oh, what? Oh, nothing, that's very interesting, that's all, I said, and I thought oh—

JOSEPH. Don't do this to yourself.

LINDA *(walking to the mirror)*. Oh—he doesn't know, and I'm not about to tell him, but I was a smoker at eighteen, nineteen. Sure I was. Wasn't everybody?

JOSEPH. Linda.

LINDA. Alcohol? Sure! I met my husband at age twenty over a bottle of tequila, if I remember it right.

STEPHANIE *(off)*. Mom, I need to talk to you!

LINDA *(at the mirror)*. Although I don't remember too much, because there was plenty to drink in those days.

JOSEPH. Linda.

STEPHANIE *(off, knocking at the door)*. Dad, Mom, are you in there? What are you doing? Why can't I come in?

JOSEPH *(exploding)*. Yes, we're here, just give us two minutes alone! Is that too much to ask? Now go back downstairs.

LINDA *(picking up STEPHANIE's pack of cigarettes)*. And see this? I've passed it on.

JOSEPH. What are you talking about? Where did those—

LINDA. They're Stephanie's. She must have left them here this morning. I saw them in her bedroom once, but I didn't have the courage to say a thing. Ten-to-one she picked this brand because the color of the box matches an outfit. I used to smoke menthol because I thought the green box was hip.

JOSEPH. Stop it. Stop this beating yourself up. You're tired, you're in shock—

LINDA *(waving the papers at him)*. Have you read the reports?

JOSEPH. You know I have.

LINDA. I have cancer, Joe. Infiltrating ductal cancer of the breast. How romantic. Possible metastasis. Know what that means?

JOSEPH. *Possible*, they say—

LINDA. That it's spread. That it *might* have spread, at least, already.

JOSEPH. They can't say that yet for certain.

LINDA. So when you go to work tomorrow, and you look at your calendar, now, let's see, what are we doing a month, six months from now, just know— I might not even be there.

(The door swings open, and STEPHANIE walks in.)

STEPHANIE. I was going to ask—why won't anybody talk to me tonight? Why has the door been closed ever since I got home? Why won't you let me in? *(Beat.)* But now I know.

JOSEPH. Sweetheart, go back downstairs. Your mother's exhausted.

LINDA. Stephanie, I—

JOSEPH. Linda, please.

STEPHANIE. Why couldn't you talk to me, too?

(Lights fade as LINDA sits on the bed, and STEPHANIE backs away toward the door.)

SCENE 4

(Lights change as we see STEPHANIE, in her own room, alone. She looks toward the doorway, as if to listen for her parents' voices, then turns away. She steps into the room and walks toward a doll—or perhaps it is a stuffed animal, a soft and fuzzy bear. She picks it up, looks at it, and sits down on a chair or bed, holding the bear in front of her, facing her. She talks to the bear.)

STEPHANIE. Mom. *(Beat.)* I need to talk. *(Beat.)* You didn't mean that, did you, what you said to Dad? About how sick you— *(Beat.)* You can't leave now, Mother. You're all I know. What would I do? And who would want me? 'Cause now it'll happen to me, too. And if someone did want me, and if I had children, could I do this to them? *(Pause.)* I'm so angry, and so afraid. I blame you for everything. I blame you, because you're the only person on earth who might ever forgive me. I can't hate you and love you, too, Mom. Tell me what to do. *(Lights fade.)*

SCENE 5

(The family kitchen, late at night. LINDA and JOSEPH sit in their socks on either side of the table, facing out. They each have a mug, and a big cookie jar is in the

*center of the table. Near LINDA, a few pieces of paper
—the reports.)*

LINDA. I want to be angry. I want to cry. What's the matter with me? It's like I've been shot in the street— I'm
lying on my back, I'm dying in the street but I feel no
pain. And everyone is walking past me, they don't even
know. This is some dream. I'm going to wake up and
this all will have happened to someone else, not me.
They've made a mistake, they must have. It isn't me.

JOSEPH. It's a simple procedure. That's what they said. It
might even be outpatient—that's what they thought.

LINDA. That's what they thought on Monday, Joe.

JOSEPH. I know.

LINDA *(pulling a piece of paper from the pile).* They
faxed me this, you know. I don't suppose it was meant
to come out of somebody else's machine.

JOSEPH. They've found more. But now they know what
they're dealing with, they'll go in and get it out. You'll
be as good as new.

LINDA. That's what you said on Monday. What do you
tell me tomorrow, if the news is even worse? *(Beat. She
puts down the paper.)* I can't even look at this. I've gone
from demanding to know it all, to not wanting to hear a
thing. I don't want to know, I don't want to think about
it. I took the long way home today just so I wouldn't
have to drive past the hospital. A doctor came on the TV
to sell me aspirin, I threw the remote control at the set.

JOSEPH. It's all right. Do you want something? I could get
you something, make you something. Some more tea, a
cookie—they're chocolate chip—

LINDA. Know something? This is how sick this really is ... The last few years— I don't even like cookies. I don't. I make them—for you, the kids—but I don't eat them. They taste like butter—awful. I've grown to actually like the taste of carrots. I taste the juice from a tomato or the crunch of celery and I think, God, this is glorious. Grains and rice and everything good for you and I eat that stuff now and I love it, it's all a big ice cream sundae to me. I teach a classroom of kids on fire with energy and I'm with them all the way. I swim, I run. I take the stairs when I can, I walk when I could ride. This should happen to someone else. Things like this don't happen to people like me.

JOSEPH. I know that. I love you.

LINDA. When my father died—he was forty pounds too big, for years, and the way he ate—he was a bull, but it was all bottled up inside, his face was so red and you could just feel the pressure in his blood. You knew it would happen—what he had done to his heart—and that day it did—a summer day, a little hot, and down he went like you knew he would, he just dropped onto the driveway, crumpled on the blacktop, and my mother screamed, and we cried but you knew it would happen. My mother—

JOSEPH. Had cancer. Like you. It surprised her, too—

LINDA. But *lung*. *Lung* cancer, Joe. And she smoked a pack a day for thirty-five years straight— Lucky Strike, 'cause she liked the name—and I can't believe I'm saying such a horrible thing, but it's true ... she deserved it. What a horrible thing for a daughter to say, but it's true. She deserved more—she only lost half a lung—a week later, back on her feet. She was lucky. But why me?

JOSEPH. But you'll make it. You'll fight it. The doctor told you, it isn't a death sentence anymore. *(Pause.)* Did you talk to Stephanie?

LINDA. I did, again, today. And she wants to be so tough. She wants to hold *me* up. She wants to be there tomorrow, the hospital, the surgery, but I can't make her do that. And I look in her eyes and she's trying so hard, and I think, what have I done to my daughter? You know what this means, the statistics. Someday *she'll* sit at a table with reports in her hand and explain to her kids, I may not be here next month, next week, but buck up, kids, keep that smile on your face.

JOSEPH. You'll be here. Next week, next month. You'll be here. You'll fight it.

(STEPHANIE's face appears in the doorway behind them, hiding. She is fully dressed, and carries a backpack.)

LINDA. This can't be. It can't be that my children will grow up and I won't be there to see them. That Nicky walks across the stage a college graduate and I'm not there. That he cheers his son at Little League and there's no me. That Stephanie gets married and you walk her down the aisle but there's no Linda, she's not there.

(STEPHANIE reacts.)

And Stephanie bears a child, that baby screams and cries with the joy of life but I don't get to hear a thing.

JOSEPH *(takes her hand).* Let's go. *(STEPHANIE retreats from view.)* Let's go upstairs. You need sleep, and I'll hold you close.

(They rise, slowly, and leave through the doorway, JOSEPH's arm around LINDA. Beat. STEPHANIE slides back into the room, not making a sound, and searches. She rummages through some things, finds a key, and puts it in her pocket. Then she looks again—in cabinets, in the fridge—then sees the cookie jar. She quickly unloads the entire jar into the outer pocket of her backpack. Then looks again and finds a pencil. Looking for paper, she sees the reports. She picks up a page, looks at it, holds back her reaction and quickly puts it face down on the table. She feverishly writes a note on the back, puts down the pencil, then looks at the note. She kisses the note softly, her eyes closed, holding back tears, then puts the note on the table, grabs her backpack, looks behind her, and runs—flies—off. Lights fade.)

SCENE 6

(Operating room, in a strange and inhuman light. NURSE, in surgical gown and mask, enters. She walks quickly to a table where she urgently arranges scalpels and instruments. NURSE'S AIDE, in gown and mask, follows behind, and readies equipment. STEPHANIE, in her regular clothes, wanders in, unsure of why she's there.)

NURSE. Doctor, where have you been?

NURSE'S AIDE. We've been waiting. The patient…is
   critical.
NURSE. Scrub.

   (*NURSE and NURSE'S AIDE take STEPHANIE's hands
   and quickly go through the motions of scrubbing them.*)

NURSE'S AIDE. Gloves.
STEPHANIE. Why are you— (*They shove her hands into
   surgical gloves.*)
NURSE. Gown. (*They quickly dress her with the gown.*)
NURSE'S AIDE. Mask.
STEPHANIE. No, I—

   (*They cover her mouth with the mask, as she begins to
   struggle. ORDERLY enters, quickly.*)

ORDERLY. Is the doctor here?
NURSE & NURSE'S AIDE. Yes.
STEPHANIE (*simultaneously*). No, I—
NURSE & NURSE'S AIDE. Yes. Quickly—the patient.

   (*They take STEPHANIE, resisting but too confused to
   fight, to center. ORDERLY wheels on a prone LINDA,
   who wears a hospital gown, on an operating cart. She is
   wheeled in front of STEPHANIE, as STEPHANIE turns
   and sees her. NURSE, NURSE'S AIDE and ORDERLY
   produce instruments in rapid succession.*)

STEPHANIE. Mother, I—
NURSE. Scalpel.
NURSE'S AIDE. Knife.

NURSE. Laser.
NURSE'S AIDE. Knife.
STEPHANIE. Mother, Grandma, Daddy, I don't—
ORDERLY. Doctor, quickly! The patient!
NURSE. Cut.
NURSE'S AIDE. Knife.
ORDERLY. Cut.
STEPHANIE. I can't do this—you don't understand!
NURSE. The patient!
NURSE'S AIDE. Doctor!
NURSE. Is dying!
STEPHANIE. No! *(She rips the mask from her face.)*
ORDERLY. Doctor!
NURSE. Scalpel.
NURSE'S AIDE. Cut.
NURSE. Scalpel.
NURSE'S AIDE. Cut.
NURSE. Knife!

(They thrust the knife into STEPHANIE's hands. She stands over her mother, knife in hand.)

STEPHANIE. You don't understand. I don't know how to ... I can't...
ORDERLY. Doctor, please!
NURSE'S AIDE. The patient!
ORDERLY. Dying!
NURSE. Dying!
NURSE'S AIDE. Cut!
NURSE. The breast!
NURSE'S AIDE. Knife!
ORDERLY. Cut!

(As STEPHANIE reaches toward her mother with the knife, she freezes, drops the knife, and begins to rip the gloves from her hands.)

ORDERLY. Doctor, what are you doing? The patient!

NURSE. Dying!

STEPHANIE. I can't do this. *(She throws her gown to the floor.)*

ORDERLY. Doctor!

LINDA *(rising, and looking at STEPHANIE)*. Doctor, save me. Who else can save me?

STEPHANIE *(backing away)*. Mother, forgive me. Mommy, please. I want to. I can't. I don't know how—

ORDERLY. The patient!

NURSE. Will die.

NURSE'S AIDE. Die!

STEPHANIE. I can't do it! *(Backing away.)* Forgive me, Mommy, please!

(ORDERLY briskly wheels LINDA off, NURSE'S AIDE follows, as STEPHANIE staggers back into a sofa. GRANDMA circles back to the sofa, and in her regular clothes, holds STEPHANIE, who is sobbing. New light. The living room at Grandma's house.)

SCENE 7

GRANDMA. There, now.

STEPHANIE. Mommy, please, God...

GRANDMA. There, now. What happened?

STEPHANIE. Save her!

GRANDMA. Princess.

STEPHANIE. I saw her— I was there—the knife!

GRANDMA. A dream? Hold tight to Grandma—there, there. You're with your grandma at Grandma's house. What a horrible dream...

STEPHANIE. I'm going!

GRANDMA. Where? Where are you going?

STEPHANIE *(pulling herself up, pulling herself together, to go)*. I'm going now.

GRANDMA. Oh, are you?

STEPHANIE. *(beginning to leave)*. I can't leave her there. I'm going.

GRANDMA. And what will you do when you get there?

STEPHANIE. I... I will...

GRANDMA. Are you a doctor?

STEPHANIE *(pause)*. Yes.

GRANDMA. Oh, I see. That's nice.

STEPHANIE. Yes, if I have to be, I am. Goodbye.

GRANDMA. Goodbye. *(Beat. Calling after her.)* I hope you're a better doctor than you were a runaway.

STEPHANIE *(turning, sharply)*. What's that?

GRANDMA. I said... I hope you're a little better at performing surgery than you were at running away from home.

STEPHANIE. How dare you say that.

GRANDMA. Say what?

STEPHANIE. You don't understand me, Grandma.

GRANDMA. I have two beautiful grandchildren. I am so proud of them. I tell my friends all about them.

STEPHANIE. What are you talking about.

GRANDMA. My grandson Nicky, he's a scientist, I tell them. "Oh," my friends say. He won a contest at school! "Really! That's something!"

STEPHANIE. I'm leaving now.

GRANDMA. And my granddaughter—so wonderful—she runs away from home! "Well, that's impressive." Yes, she's really something! "How far did she get? Havana? Paris? Rome?" Six blocks, I will tell them!

STEPHANIE. Yeah, well I...

GRANDMA. So upset. A runaway. And how far did you get? Six blocks! To your grandma's house!

STEPHANIE. Yeah, I...know.

GRANDMA. And you didn't even make it inside last night—just the porch!

STEPHANIE. I didn't want to wake you.

GRANDMA. When was it? So early! I woke up—it was still dark—the cat had been outside, to catch the mice, and he was scratching the door. I get up, open the door, in comes Fufi, and I see my princess tight asleep on the porch swing, with the doormat on top of her like a blanket! Look, Fufi, I say, there's the princess on the porch! I know, says Fufi, that's why I scratch the door to wake you up! I try to wake her up, too, but she's sleeping! Fufi, I say, why didn't she come inside? They *have* a key! Fufi says, I don't know!

STEPHANIE. I took the key. Then I lost it.

GRANDMA. Just then the phone rings. Who can it be, I say, it's early! It's Joseph. Have you seen Steffi, he says. Have you seen her at all? Of course, I say. She's on my porch. Fufi found her on the swing. Thank God, he says—that's all he say, thank God.

STEPHANIE. I didn't mean it.

GRANDMA. I woke up, he says, with a funny feeling. Like a door was open or something was wrong. I go downstairs and in the hall by the door I see someone dropped three cookies—chocolate chip—and the key to Grandma's house. I look upstairs— Nicky, yes. No Steffi. So I call you. Thank God.

STEPHANIE. I didn't mean to hurt anybody. I was so afraid.

GRANDMA. He called me from the basement so your poor mother wouldn't wake up and be afraid. Such a nice man.

STEPHANIE. I'm going to save her, Grandma.

GRANDMA. Steffi—

STEPHANIE. I am. I don't know how, but I am.

GRANDMA. You're my little princess. Don't work yourself up like that.

STEPHANIE. No one thinks I can. No one even cares.

GRANDMA (*getting up*). Don't worry yourself so hard, little Steffi. Lie back down for your grandma and rest. (*STEPHANIE sinks back down.*) Take a rest, now, and later—warm milk from your grandmother's kitchen. Rest, now ...

STEPHANIE. They can't stop me. They can't.

SCENE 8

(*Just as she relaxes back and her eyes close, the lights change as the phone rings, loudly. STEPHANIE springs up to answer it.*)

STEPHANIE. Doctor? Yes, I'm here!

(DOCTOR appears, with a phone in his hand. He speaks into the receiver.)

DOCTOR. Procedure patient, doctor no.
STEPHANIE. The patient, yes! Tell me doctor, how is—

(ADMINISTRATOR appears, also with a phone.)

ADMINISTRATOR. Press five for doctor. Is this the patient to whom I am speaking?
STEPHANIE. Yes! No! But I know the patient, I need to—
ADMINISTRATOR. If so, press two. If not, access is not available at this time.
STEPHANIE. I need to know, I need to know now, how is she—
DOCTOR. Bleeding patient suture cut.

(CHAPLAIN appears in clerical collar, with a phone.)

CHAPLAIN. At this time, we must all—
ADMINISTRATOR. Press three for insurance. Press four for unauthorized procedures.
STEPHANIE. Stop this. One of you—tell me—
DOCTOR. Patient sickness.
CHAPLAIN. Rely on faith. Draw strength from—
ADMINISTRATOR. Beeeep. Your request is not valid. Your access is denied.
CHAPLAIN. Scripture.
DOCTOR. Bleeding cut.
STEPHANIE. The patient...is my mother. My very own—
ADMINISTRATOR. If this is not the patient, simply hang up. Or press "pound" for more options.

STEPHANIE. Pound! Pound!

CHAPLAIN. We can all feel angry.

DOCTOR. Ductal tissue node lymph.

ADMINISTRATOR. We're sorry. Your request is not valid.

CHAPLAIN. We needn't blame ourselves—

DOCTOR. Mastectomy cut!

STEPHANIE. Someone! Tell me!

ADMINISTRATOR. Press two.

CHAPLAIN For feeling alone.

STEPHANIE. Someone!

DOCTOR. Bleeding!

STEPHANIE. Someone, tell me!

ADMINISTRATOR. For terminal cases—

CHAPLAIN. Faith!

ADMINISTRATOR. Press one.

STEPHANIE. Somebody tell me where she is and what has happened! *(No response.)* Tell me! *(Nothing.)* Is she even alive?

(In rhythmic succession, the phones slam: Click, click, click. DOCTOR, ADMINISTRATOR and CHAPLAIN exit in a line.)

SCENE 9

(STEPHANIE steps forward and lights change, as NICK and JOSEPH fill in behind her, each bringing an undersized wooden chair as found in young children's classrooms. MR. JOHNSON, a kind-looking teacher, stands to the side. STEPHANIE faces front as she speaks.)

STEPHANIE. And we thought you'd really want to know. I mean, she's been gone a couple of days now, so you're probably worried. I mean, she's your teacher. So I asked my dad—that's him—and he asked Mr. Johnson here. And he said sure, and I thought that was a pretty cool thing for a substitute teacher to do. I mean, for a substitute. Let's face it—like he could have done like usual and just shown you the movie. But he said OK, so we came here. *(She looks at NICK and JOSEPH, then back front.)* Your teacher— my mother—is a little sick. It's a disease called ... cancer ... that's what she's got ... and she went to the hospital. You know the big buildings across the river, by the baseball park? That's where she is. And this disease—sickness—cancer—is caused by a lot of things. Like bad things you eat ...

NICK. Steph.

STEPHANIE. Or drink, or smoke.

NICK. Um, Stephanie ...

STEPHANIE. Hardly anybody ever gets it, but it can happen—

NICK. Steph!

STEPHANIE *(looking at him).* Um, this is like my brother.

NICK. Hi.

STEPHANIE. He's going to talk to you ...

(NICK pulls out a thick stack of note cards.)

About the science part.

NICK. Right. Thanks. *(He reads from the first card.)* Breast cancer ... is the uncontrolled growth of cells, likely caused by a combination of genes, mutated by carcinogens, in tissue conducive to spread. *(He looks up, then reads again.)* More than one woman in ten will contract the disease during her lifetime— *(He looks up.)* —though more than seventy percent of those have none of the standard risk factors in their— *(He looks up, and stops.)* You can't understand that, can you. *(Beat.)* Sorry. *(Beat. He puts the note cards back in his pocket. Pause.)* Have you ever been to the doctor, anybody? *(He looks.)* I thought so. And if you went there because you were sick, you kinda wondered why—why it happened to you. And sometimes they know—this disease, breast cancer, they think sometimes maybe you get it because someone in your family had it. But other things are part of it, too—like drinking too much, smoking, not exercising, and eating too much fat in your food—and even some things that don't seem like they should matter— like how tall you are or when you have your first baby. But sometimes, they just don't know. The doctors and nurses, they can't always tell you. So I guess it's up to you to lead a healthy life. And if you do get sick, the doctors and nurses will do the best they can. But sometimes people get very sick, and they can't always help you. *(Beat.)* That's what I know. Thanks for listening to me.

(NICK sits back down, as JOSEPH puts his hand on NICK's shoulder. STEPHANIE steps forward.)

STEPHANIE. That's my brother. His name is Nick. And he's pretty smart sometimes. *(Beat.)* But he's wrong about the last part. Nothing bad is going to happen to

her. Because it just can't. And that's what I came here to
tell you. It just can't. She's my mother.

(JOSEPH stands, and lights fade.)

SCENE 10

*(The family home. As lights come up, NICK is on a
chair, trying to hang the other end of a hand-lettered
banner saying, "Welcome Home, Mom." STEPHANIE is
setting the table.)*

NICK. Hand me the tape. Over there.

STEPHANIE. I'm busy.

NICK. Just reach for the tape—I can't get it from here.

STEPHANIE *(stopping)*. We agreed that all this would be
done by six o'clock. I gave you like three things to do.
That's all I asked.

NICK. And I'm doin' 'em! Hand me the tape.

STEPHANIE. Dad said they'll be back by six-thirty.
You've got about three minutes to hold up your end.

NICK. I'm holding it—can't you see me?

STEPHANIE. Listen, Nick. I've spent the day on this. I
went to the library to study what she should eat. I went
to the store to get it. And then I came home to cook it.

NICK. You can't cook.

STEPHANIE. I cleaned house starting this morning—as
soon as Dad got the call saying she'd be coming—and
yeah, I cooked this meal because I love her and when
she walks through that door I don't want her to lift a
finger. I want her to think she's the Queen of the World.

NICK. Well, that's great, Steph. *(Getting off the chair, letting the banner droop.)* That's really great. Because it's the first time since Mom got sick that you've done a thing. Do you know that? When she first got sick—the two of you got home that day, from the doctor—you *fought* with her. For ruining *your* day. I couldn't believe it. Our mother's so sick, and you're the one that's screaming. And if it wasn't that, it was you, collapsed in the corner, crying for sympathy, so she'd come make *you* feel better. Or running away. Running away, for Chrissakes, when she needs us.

STEPHANIE. I tried. I tried everything I could think of. I tried to help, but nothing I did was right. No one would believe I could help her. I tried—

NICK. You've never done a thing. And when Dad needed help, he came to *me*. Her first night in the hospital, and he knocks on my door at like one or two in the morning and says he's got to talk to somebody, he knows he can't upset Stephanie, so can we talk. And I'd never seen him cry in my life, and that was the night. And he just kind of shook on the bed when it happened. And he came to *me*. *(Beat.)* So get over yourself. *(Pause, then NICK storms out, just as the doorbell rings.)* Get over here!

(They rush into place— STEPHANIE grabs the party hats and blowers and tooters and throws NICK his share and NICK leaps on the chair, holding up the banner as STEPHANIE opens the door.)

NICK & STEPHANIE *(with blowers, tooters and voices).* TA-DAAAAAAA!!!

(GRANDMA enters, triumphantly.)

GRANDMA. Ta-da is right! Bingo! What a party! Where's
  my special girl? The guest of honor! *(To STEPHANIE.)* I
  like your hat!

STEPHANIE. She isn't here yet, Grandma. We thought
  you were her.

GRANDMA. Then I'm early! Bingo! *(She grabs a hat and
  blower.)*

NICK. Hey, Grandma.

GRANDMA. Nicky! *(She blows.)*

NICK *(tossing the tape to STEPHANIE)*. Here, Sister. Tape
  yourself. *(He leaves.)*

GRANDMA. What's with him? *(Beat.)*

STEPHANIE. I'm an idiot, Grandma. I'm no good.

GRANDMA. Not that again. Princess...

STEPHANIE. I need a drink.

GRANDMA. You're too young now, Stephanie. Maybe
  later, when your mother gets home. Champagne!

STEPHANIE. If I'm too young for a drink, then a cigarette.
  I need a cigarette.

*(GRANDMA sits by STEPHANIE, reaches into her
purse, pulls out a pack of cigarettes, and offers it to
STEPHANIE.)*

GRANDMA. Here.

STEPHANIE *(startled)*. Grandma! What's that?

GRANDMA. A pack of cigarettes. Lucky Strike. You want
  one?

STEPHANIE. Grandma, you can't do that—you had...can-
  cer! Lung cancer! You can't smoke—you don't smoke!

GRANDMA. Of course I don't. Do you?

STEPHANIE. No, I—I don't ... with friends ... a couple of ... maybe sometimes, I ... don't.

GRANDMA. I should hope not. They'll kill you, cigarettes. You know that?

STEPHANIE. Of course I do.

GRANDMA. When I got sick—awful sick, I couldn't breathe—to the hospital I go. And the doctor, a nice man—he's a specialist—he specialize in cancer—and he fix me up. What a nice man. And after the operation, I feel good, I can breathe just fine, so I want a cigarette. The nurse—she didn't like me too much—she didn't like me, and I didn't like her—she said no. A couple of days of that, and I think, who is she to tell me what to do? To tell me what I can have and what I can't have in my life. I want my cigarettes, so I get my purse, I walk out of the room, I get in the elevator and go. And I walk out the door, across the park and all the way back to the neighborhood. Home. And I bought this pack of Lucky Strike on the way. I got home, I thought, that feels better. I looked at the cigarettes, I thought, who wants to smoke these? They'll kill you! That was—what—what is today—twenty—twenty-two years ago. Same pack. And I never smoked since. But they're still in my purse. And if I don't want to do something, I don't do it. And if I do, I do. And I don't blame anybody. Because it's my life.

STEPHANIE. Right, Grandma.

GRANDMA. So don't smoke, Princess. But if you ever need to not have a cigarette, you can come and not have one of mine.

STEPHANIE. Thanks, Grandma. I actually think I know what you mean.

(NICK comes flying down the stairs, shouting.)

NICK. They're coming! I see the van! They're coming!
STEPHANIE *(jumping up).* Quick, Grandma—here!

(They all jump into place—hats, blowers, and NICK holds the sign.)

NICK, STEPHANIE & GRANDMA. TA-DAAAAAAA!!!

(The door opens, and JOSEPH enters, alone. He is very tired. He stands with the keys in his hand.)

JOSEPH. Children. Grandmother. *(Beat.)* Don't be afraid. Nick, Stephanie, your mother is alive. But she's a very sick woman. I couldn't bring her home. They wouldn't begin to let me. *(Pause.)*
STEPHANIE. Then what are we doing here? *(She stands, and then goes to JOSEPH and takes the keys from his hand.)* We're going. Let's go.

(She goes, and they follow, hats still on their heads and party favors in their hands. NICK pulls the banner behind him, bringing it along.)

SCENE 11

(They move directly to the minivan. They've been driving for a few minutes when the lights come up, STEPHANIE at the wheel, and JOSEPH in front beside her. NICK and GRANDMA in back.)

STEPHANIE. So why wouldn't they let you?

JOSEPH. What?

STEPHANIE. Take her.

JOSEPH. Metastaphithus. It's still possible. They're testing. And she took a bad turn—she's so weak.

NICK. Metastasis, Dad.

GRANDMA. What?

NICK. Spread of cancer to another organ, usually through the blood.

JOSEPH. Yes, Nick. You're right.

STEPHANIE. But shouldn't they know? By now?

NICK. They must be doing staging.

GRANDMA. What's he talking about?

NICK. Staging—I looked it up—the tumors and lymph nodes, positive and negative.

STEPHANIE. Why don't they know? These doctors don't know what they're doing!

JOSEPH. The oncologist says—

GRANDMA. Berta says—

NICK. Grandma, what does Berta know? This is real. We should listen to the oncologist.

GRANDMA. Oncologist? We should listen to a man who straightens teeth?

NICK. Not orthodontist, Grandma, oncolo—

GRANDMA. Listen once to Berta.

STEPHANIE. We're listening, Grandma. Go ahead.

GRANDMA. Berta says...there's a new way with cancer. If I'd have known, years ago, no operation, no hospital, I wouldn't even have gotten sick. Because nowadays, the secret is this...they eat the cartilage of...

NICK. Here we go.

GRANDMA. The shark. Shark cartilage. And do you know why?

JOSEPH. Why, Grandmother.

GRANDMA. Sharks—no matter how long they live—hundreds of years...

NICK. Sharks don't live hundreds of years, Grandma.

GRANDMA. No matter how long they live—they never get cancer, says Berta. Heart attack, like Grandpa, maybe. Maybe a little ar-tritis, like me. But cancer? Never.

STEPHANIE. Grandma...

GRANDMA. What do I know? I'm just saying—Berta says.

STEPHANIE *(slowing the van)*. We're here.

JOSEPH. That's her window—second from the top, third from the left.

NICK. It's dark. *(The van stops.)*

STEPHANIE. Do you think she's awake? Is she in pain?

NICK. We should listen to the doctors.

GRANDMA. We should pray. We should be storming heaven with our prayers.

JOSEPH. We'll do all those things. I think she is in pain, or she was, when I was here before. She has the drugs she can use for the pain, but she doesn't want to. She wants to be awake. And alive and at home, with us. And I hope she'll be fine. But you have to be prepared—Nicky, Steffi—for whatever happens.

STEPHANIE. I won't think that way, Daddy. I just won't.

(They get out of the van. Lights fade.)

SCENE 12

(The waiting room. Two a.m. Dim light. Four chairs, with JOSEPH and GRANDMA on either end, asleep. JOSEPH is sprawled, his head lolling back and his mouth wide open. He occasionally snores. A party favor sticks out of his pocket. GRANDMA sits upright, tightly bunched, with her arms folded across her chest and her head leaning forward. Her party hat is still on. NICK and STEPHANIE are in the two middle chairs, wide awake, facing out. The "Welcome Home, Mom" banner is tangled on the chairs behind them.)

STEPHANIE. So like, if Mom dies, will you be my friend?

NICK. What kind of question is that? You're scaring me. Don't think that way.

STEPHANIE. All right. *(Beat.)*

NICK. So what day is it?

STEPHANIE. Um ... I don't know. Clueless.

NICK. Me, too. How long has she been here?

STEPHANIE. Not long. It just seems that way. *(Beat.)* So will you? If Mom dies, will you be my friend?

NICK. Don't talk that way. What if she lives? Would you want me to be your friend then? *(Pause.)* Well?

STEPHANIE. Well, then it's just normal, so ... *(Beat.)* Yeah. I would. I do. I need you, either way. She stays or goes, I need you.

NICK. Yeah well ... me, too. You *are* my friend. You always were.

STEPHANIE. Yeah, well ... thanks. *(Beat.)* Nick.

NICK *(beat)*. Hey Stephanie. It's Saturday, right?

STEPHANIE. Maybe ... yeah, why?

NICK. It's October, third week. It's Saturday night.

STEPHANIE. It's almost Sunday morning.

NICK. Guess what this is.

STEPHANIE. What.

NICK *(beat)*. It's Homecoming.

STEPHANIE. Oh... Wow...

NICK. Happy Homecoming. Would you like to dance?

STEPHANIE. That's so wild. Well, hey, I guess I got what I wanted!

NICK. Like...

STEPHANIE. The homecoming stuff! I mean, I got a date.

NICK. Yeah...

STEPHANIE. With a guy...

NICK. Right...

STEPHANIE. I'm out late ...

NICK. Sure.

STEPHANIE. Doing things I've never done before...

NICK. Yeah...

STEPHANIE *(looking at GRANDMA)*. And it's really been a wild party—I mean, some of us still have our party hats!

NICK *(putting his arm around her)*. Yeah, well... Happy Homecoming. *(Pause.)*

STEPHANIE. Oh, Mom... Please please don't go. *(Lights fade.)*

SCENE 13

(In the transition from the previous scene, JOSEPH, NICK and GRANDMA leave the waiting room and slowly walk toward DC, led by JOSEPH. STEPHANIE follows behind, not a part of their group, and unsure of

*why they are there. As they begin this move, we see
LINDA enter the parents' bedroom. Throughout her
speech, LINDA watches STEPHANIE, almost speaking
to her, as LINDA sets up the dressing table, etc., creat-
ing the home for STEPHANIE to return to.)*

LINDA. I remember the day we brought you home, your
father and I.

*(As she continues, it becomes clear to the audience, and
to STEPHANIE, that JOSEPH, NICK and GRANDMA
are visiting a grave. Perhaps NICK carries unseen flow-
ers, and as each person approaches the grave and
kneels, they take their individual flower from NICK,
bring it to their nose, and gently cast it onto the grave.
Silent thoughts from each. Perhaps a silent prayer from
GRANDMA.)*

And you were so small. How could something so tiny be
so full of life and hope. And we were transformed.
Nothing was the same from that moment on. *(Pause.)*
That night, you slept in our bed, up against me, and I
woke to feel you feeding at my breast, and it really felt
like we were one—you—and me—and your father—and
all the world. *(Beat. Moving toward them.)* And that has
never stopped. So be strong, Stephanie. Now that I'm
gone, be strong.

STEPHANIE *(as she approaches the group around the
grave)*. Whose funeral is this? Whose grave is this?
LINDA *(going to her, reaching out)*. It's my grave, dear
Stephanie. It's mine.

STEPHANIE *(trying to back away, talking directly to LINDA).* No. I don't know this person. I've never met this person before in my life.

LINDA. Stephanie.

STEPHANIE. How dare you do this to me. How dare you leave me.

LINDA. Little Steffi.

STEPHANIE. How could you bring me here.

LINDA. Steffi.

STEPHANIE. How could you bring me into this world, just to leave me.

JOSEPH. Stephanie. Your mother.

STEPHANIE. You're not my mother. Go. *(As she runs away.)* Go!

(STEPHANIE runs from the group, back toward the bedroom, as the group files away, LINDA in one direction, the others in another. STEPHANIE collapses into the bedroom, as lights change.)

SCENE 14

(As before, with just the hint of new morning light. STEPHANIE is deep asleep on the bed. LINDA enters, carrying a bag with clothing. She walks haltingly, but looks for and sees STEPHANIE, and smiles. She sets her bag down, and approaches the bed.)

LINDA *(softly).* Stephanie! *(She sits on the bed and touches STEPHANIE.)* Stephanie.

STEPHANIE *(waking).* Huh?

LINDA. Stephanie—it's morning.

STEPHANIE *(waking).* What? Where am I?

LINDA *(reaching toward her).* You're in your mom and dad's room, like a little kid.

STEPHANIE. Where are you? Is it you?

LINDA. Yes, it's me. I'm right here.

STEPHANIE. Oh, Mama... *(She hugs LINDA.)*

LINDA. Careful. Ouch. Here—this side, my good side. There.

STEPHANIE. Oh, Mama. Oh, my God. *(She hugs LINDA harder.)*

LINDA. Not too tight. I have holes—I might leak. You look awful. Were you crying?

STEPHANIE. I had dreams, nightmares.

LINDA. My poor baby.

STEPHANIE. Last night I saw you— I thought I saw you—you weren't living anymore. And I felt the most terrible things. And I said the most terrible things.

LINDA. Here, now.

STEPHANIE. But you're here. Are you all right, will you—

LINDA. I think I'll be fine. They can't tell me that for sure, but that's the way these things work. Your father spent the night at the hospital again last night and we drove home this morning as soon as they'd let us. And I'll go back for radiation and chemotherapy and ta-moxifen and treatments and who knows what. But they think I'll be fine and I've decided I'll think so, too. And if it ever comes back, I'll fight that, too.

STEPHANIE. Oh, my God. I need you, That dream— I woke up here, in this room, panting, like I'd been running down a hill. And then I cried until my eyes were dry—I couldn't make any tears—just crying.

LINDA. Stephanie. At the hospital, the whole time, I could only think of you. Be strong for Stephanie, I said.

STEPHANIE. And then I—it must have been here, it had to be—I sank back into this dream. Only this time not gray and dark and black—it was full of color. And I... was a woman, like you.

LINDA. Yes.

STEPHANIE. And I had children, like you, and a husband. Who loved me just like we love you. And I was so happy.

LINDA. Yes.

STEPHANIE. And I rose up. And from way up high I could see myself, in this bed, and I could see you in the hospital. And I could see the future—that woman who was me. And then it hit me.

LINDA. What, honey?

STEPHANIE. A terrible thing to say, but a wonderful thing to feel—that if you ever left me—if you ever did—the earth would shake, but I would still stand. I... would... make it. *(Beat.)* And then I thought, that's it! *That's* what you gave me. The gift. How to live and love and give, so that someday someone gets that gift from me. And then I thought oh please God just give me the chance to thank her. *(She hugs LINDA.)*

GRANDMA *(off)*. Linda! Stephanie!

LINDA. Well, you got that chance. Bless you.

GRANDMA *(off)*. Breakfast!

STEPHANIE. Breakfast—I'm starving!

LINDA *(getting up)*. Then we'll go. Grandma's cooking.

STEPHANIE. And Mom...I want something healthy.

LINDA *(rubbing STEPHANIE's head as she turns to go).*
Of course you do.

(GRANDMA enters in an apron, with a spatula in one hand and a stick of butter in the other.)

GRANDMA. Princess! And my Linda! I made special for you—big thick waffles, with hot melted butter. A little sprinkle of chocolate, and to top it off...whipped cream!
LINDA *(smiling at STEPHANIE).*Thank you, Mother.
GRANDMA. And bacon on the side!
LINDA. Wonderful.

(LINDA and GRANDMA leave. STEPHANIE remains, and sees the bag that LINDA brought. She sees her mother's hospital gown on top. She picks it up carefully, letting the gown unfold in her hands, then brings it in front of her body. In the mirror, she studies her image in the gown.)

LINDA *(off).* Stephanie!

(She carefully gathers the gown, brings it up to her face and kisses it. Then sets it gently back on the bag.)

LINDA *(off).* Stephanie, love, come down!
STEPHANIE *(happily).* OK, OK! *(She takes the gold jacket from the chair, slips it on, looks at the mirror, and tosses her head back in a wide, laughing smile. Lights fade.)*

CURTAIN—END OF PLAY

DIRECTOR'S NOTES

DIRECTOR'S NOTES

DIRECTOR'S NOTES

DIRECTOR'S NOTES

DIRECTOR'S NOTES